JAMES A. BAILEY

The Genius Behind the Barnum & Bailey Circus

Gloria G. Adams

Slanted Ink, Stow, OH

Other books by the author...
Ah-Choo!, with Lana Wayne Koehler, Sterling Children's Books, 2016.
Violent Video Games and Society, Greenhaven Press, 2017.
Coping with Sexism and Misogyny, Rosen, 2018.
Photo Plots: How to Write Great Photo-inspired Books and Stories, Slanted Ink, 2018.
21st Century Spaceships, Enslow Publishing, 2019.
My Underpants Are Made from Plants, with Vera J. Hurst, 2020.

Copyright © 2021 Gloria G. Adams

Publisher's Cataloging-in-Publication data

Names: Adams, Gloria G., author.
Title: James A. Bailey : the genius behind the Barnum & Bailey Circus / Gloria G. Adams.
Description: Includes bibliographical references and index. | Stow, OH: Slanted Ink, 2021. | Summary: A biography of James Anthony Bailey, world-renowned circus manager and owner of The Barnum and Bailey Greatest Show on Earth.
Identifiers: LCCN: 2021906020 | ISBN: 978-1-7367688-0-8 (hardcover) | 978-1-7367688-1-5 (paperback) | 978-1-7367688-2-2 (eBook)
Subjects: LCSH Bailey, James Anthony, 1847-1906. | Ringling Brothers Barnum and Bailey Combined Shows--History. | Circus--United States--History. | BISAC JUVENILE NONFICTION / Biography & Autobiography / Historical | JUVENILE NONFICTION / Performing Arts / Circus
Classification: LCC GV1801 .B35 A33 2021 | DDC 791.3092--dc23

All rights reserved.
This book or any portion thereof may not be reproduced or used in any manner whatsoever without the express written permission of the publisher.

Slanted Ink Stow, OH 44224
www.gloriagadams.com

Reviews for James A. Bailey...

"Authoritative, lively & entertaining, this biography is the story of James Anthony Bailey, the genius behind The Greatest Show on Earth. Middle grade readers will be drawn to the story, and to James Bailey's character, by Gloria G. Adams' quick and fluid prose. Engaging graphics point to sidebars full of historically accurate and fun information about the circus and Bailey's life. These pull young readers into the story, and into James Bailey's better qualities. James Bailey has often been overlooked by history and deserves to be recognized and honored for his many contributions."

~Margaret Maurer, Librarian
Associate Professor Emeritus
Kent State University

"P.T. Barnum has received his share of attention recently, but who was his partner in the Barnum and Bailey Circus? In *James A. Bailey: The Genius Behind the Barnum & Bailey Circus,* readers will get to know the big-hearted man who preferred to remain behind the scenes. Ms. Adams' biography makes it possible for readers to run away to join the circus, travel the world, and care for a menagerie of exotic animals, as they follow the life of the king of circus men."

~Nancy Messmore, youth services librarian

"Lions, tigers, elephants and clowns are only a few of the bright and magical images that parade through our memories as we turn the pages of this book and remember the excitement of the circus coming to town. Although his name always came last when listed with his partners, James A. Bailey truly was the quiet force behind the Greatest Show on Earth. As we follow his extraordinary life throughout these pages, we learn of Bailey's many contributions to the exciting world of the circus. It turns out, that by working hard and being kind to all, Bailey was considered by many to have been the 'Greatest Showman'. "

~Vera J. Hurst, author

Table of Contents

1. Runaway..................................2
2. A New Name..............................6
3. Civil War................................10
4. Ruth and Joe............................14
5. Australia!...............................18
6. Elephants!..............................22
7. Wild West...............................26
8. Legacy..................................30

Author's Note.............................33
Acknowledgments.........................34
Timeline..................................35
Source Notes.............................37
Photo Credits............................38
Bibliography.............................39
Index....................................41
About the Author........................42

WHAT IF...you could spend almost every day of your life at the circus?

WHAT IF...you could travel with that circus around the world, seeing sights that most people never get to see?

WHAT IF...you could hang out every day with elephants, camels, giraffes, monkeys, lions, tigers, bears, horses, and snakes?

This was the life James Anthony Bailey lived.

Born James Anthony McGinnis, he was orphaned at age 8 and changed his last name to Bailey after he joined the circus when he was just 13. He grew up to own one of the most famous circuses in the world, The Barnum and Bailey Greatest Show on Earth.

And it all happened because of a decision he made when he was just a kid, one hot summer day in Detroit, Michigan...

1 RUNAWAY

"The cops are coming!"

Jimmy McGinnis took off running when he heard his friend's warning. All the other boys scattered in different directions. Jimmy was barefoot and soaking wet from swimming in the Detroit River, which was not allowed. But a cool dip on a hot day was hard to resist.

Jimmy found a place to hide and think. Chances were, when he got home, he would be in trouble with his older sister Catherine. He'd been sent to live with her when he was only eight, right after his mother died. His father had passed away just a few years before from a disease called cholera.

Catherine made Jimmy work extra hard and punished him severely when he couldn't finish his work. He had endured her harsh treatment for years. As he sat by the river that day, Jimmy decided to take a risk that he knew would change his whole life.

CIRCUS TERMS

ABA-DABA:
Food from the cookhouse

ALFALFA:
paper money

BACK DOOR:
The performers' entrance to the Big Top

BIG TOP:
The main and largest circus tent

He slipped away and trudged down the road, barefoot, broke, and alone. Jimmy wasn't sure where he would go or what he would do. But he knew one thing: he was *not* going back home.

A farmer driving down the road gave Jimmy a ride in his wagon. When Jimmy told him he was an orphan, the farmer offered him work and a place to live.

But lifting and stacking wheat sheaves was a heavy job for a young boy. On top of that, the pay was very low.

Even though Jimmy was a hard worker, the farmer wouldn't give him a raise. Jimmy finally decided to leave. Once again, he headed out on his own, this time with a little money jingling in his pocket. He was determined, as he later said, to be "master of my own destiny."

DID YOU KNOW?

When James became a circus owner, he established "Orphan Day," one day a year when all the orphans in the city could attend the circus for free.

He was often known to carry children into the circus tent who were unable to walk and settle them into seats away from the crush of the crowd.

Circus ticket signed by James A. Bailey, Courtesy of Bridgeport History Center, Bridgeport Public Library

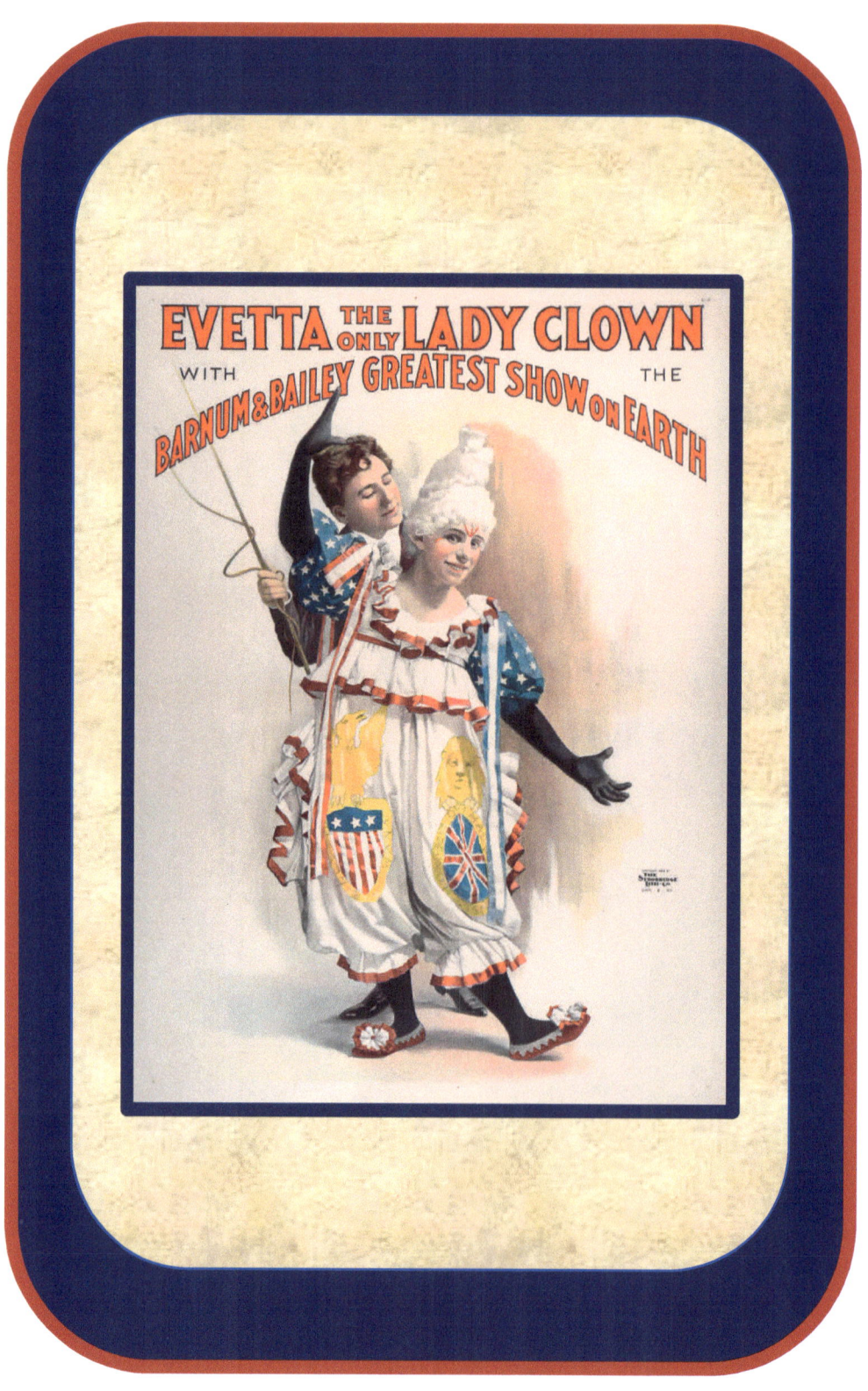

2
A NEW NAME

Ten miles from the farm, Jimmy wandered into the city of Pontiac, Michigan.

He remembered that day distinctly. "I was a boy of thirteen, the town was full of people, as a political meeting, an abolitionist rally, was being held. There were brass bands, and floats, and civic societies, and a lot of soldiers marching. It was all very wonderful to me, and I stood watching the display until I was tired."

Jimmy sat down to rest on a bench near the stables of Hodges House, one of the main hotels in Pontiac. A man who was unhitching horses said, "Say, Bub, come and help me with these horses. I'll give you a dime and your dinner."

Jimmy accepted and found a new job and a place to stay. He was "quite independent and happy" there. But on June 17, 1861, Colonel Fred H. Bailey rode into town. Jimmy's life was about to change once again.

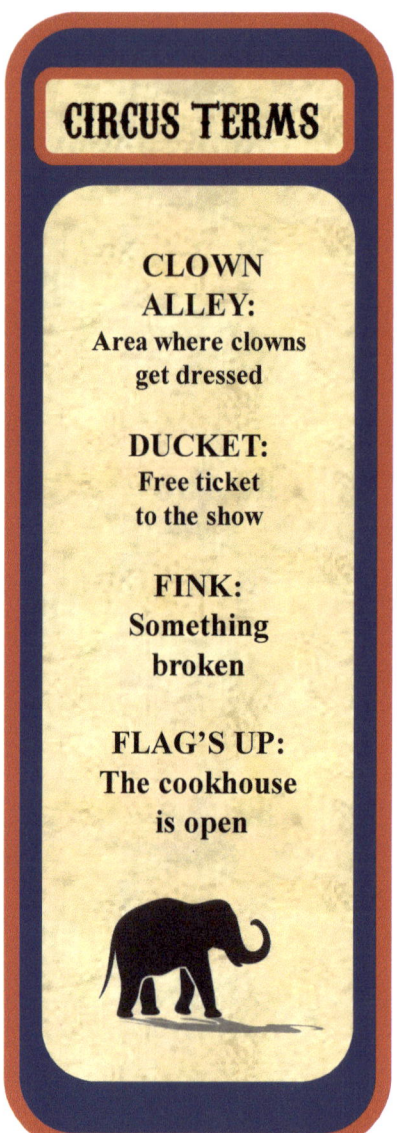

CIRCUS TERMS

CLOWN ALLEY:
Area where clowns get dressed

DUCKET:
Free ticket to the show

FINK:
Something broken

FLAG'S UP:
The cookhouse is open

Colonel Bailey was a big, slow-moving man. Jimmy described him as having "a splendid character and most kindly and generous nature."

The colonel was the general agent for John Robinson and Bill Lake's traveling circus. He, along with his advance team, had come to hang posters around town, advertising that the circus was coming to Pontiac.

Jimmy helped with the posters. He worked so hard that the colonel asked him if he would come to work for the circus. A more exciting life with better pay than the hotel? Yes!

He left with Mr. Bailey, perched on an upturned bucket in the circus wagon. Not long afterward, he took the colonel's last name. With the start of this new life, Jimmy McGinnis left not just his past, but also his name behind. From then on, he was known as James Anthony Bailey.

DID YOU KNOW?

Route Books were compiled at the end of each circus season.

They listed cities and dates when the circus performed, lists of performers, weather conditions, and any unusual events that happened during the year.

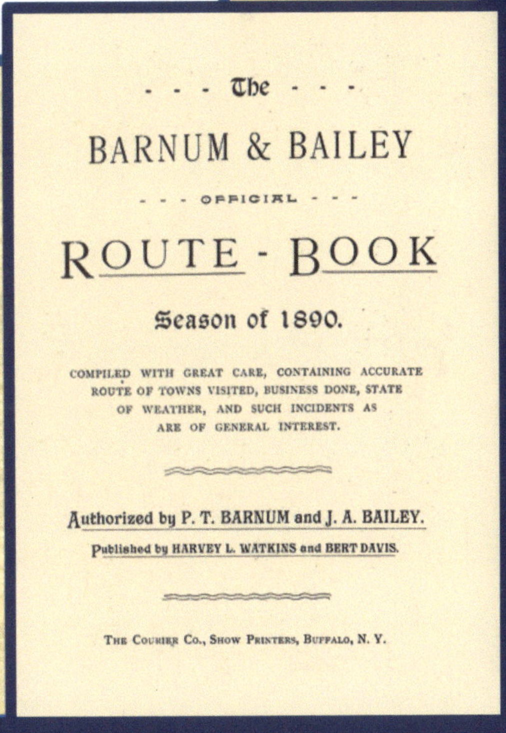

Courtesy of Milner Library, Special Collections, Illinois State University

--- The ---

BARNUM & BAILEY

--- OFFICIAL ---

ROUTE - BOOK

Season of 1890.

COMPILED WITH GREAT CARE, CONTAINING ACCURATE ROUTE OF TOWNS VISITED, BUSINESS DONE, STATE OF WEATHER, AND SUCH INCIDENTS AS ARE OF GENERAL INTEREST.

Authorized by P. T. BARNUM and J. A. BAILEY.
Published by HARVEY L. WATKINS and BERT DAVIS.

THE COURIER CO., SHOW PRINTERS, BUFFALO, N. Y.

3
CIVIL WAR

Life in the circus was very different from life at the hotel in Pontiac! James learned a lot from Colonel Bailey and Bill Lake.

He also found out that even though he was just a teenager, he still had to earn money in the off-season. The winter he was sixteen, James took a job in Nashville, Tennessee as an usher at the Nashville Theater.

One night, a man named A.H. Green came to see the show. Mr. Green was a sutler, a traveling shopkeeper who followed military battles. Sutlers sold items to the soldiers that the Army didn't provide.

The theater was packed and there were no available seats. Mr. Green offered James a bribe to get him a seat, but James refused. Sutlers were always looking for honest young men, and Mr. Green offered James a job as his clerk. James took the job. It turned out to be a dangerous one.

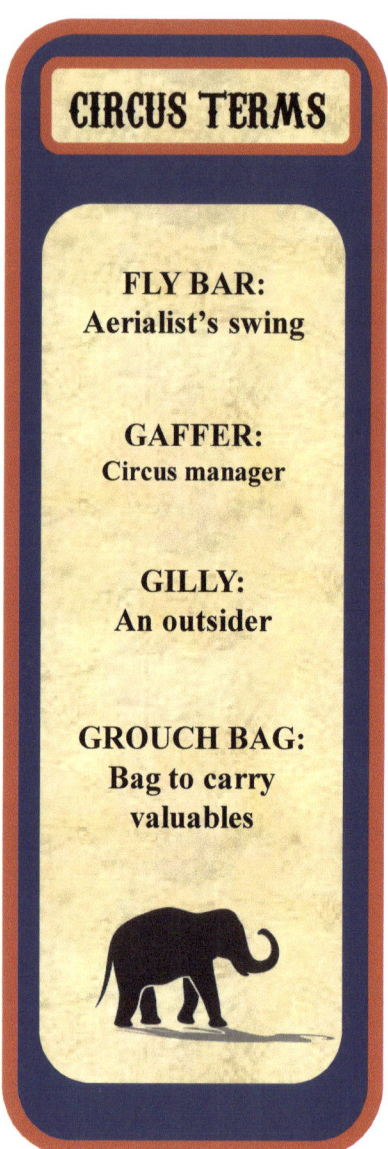

CIRCUS TERMS

FLY BAR:
Aerialist's swing

GAFFER:
Circus manager

GILLY:
An outsider

GROUCH BAG:
Bag to carry valuables

It was a time of civil war in the United States. Sutlers set up their tents close to each of the battles. One of their jobs was delivering mail to the soldiers.

One day, James ran into a battle, holding up a handful of letters. A bullet whizzed past, barely missing him and cleanly slicing off the top of one of the letters!

Mr. Green often put James in charge of the money. Once, at the Battle of Kennesaw Mountain, James was forced to stay awake in his tent all night, guarding the money. Mr. Green had left him with more than seventeen thousand dollars!

James stayed on as a sutler after the end of the war. But then one day, while on an errand for Mr. Green in Cincinnati, Ohio, James ran into his former employer, Bill Lake. Bill offered James a job. Once again, James Bailey joined the world of the circus.

DID YOU KNOW?

Sutlers not only sold everyday items, like soap, shoelaces, combs, socks, and toothbrushes, but sometimes sold unusual items like violin strings and pickled pigs' feet.

To guard their goods and money, sutlers often slept in their tents, lying on shoeboxes covered with a small mattress.

Soldiers gathered outside a sutler's tent.

4
RUTH AND JOE

James returned as an associate agent for Bill and Agnes Lake's Hippo Olympiad and Mammoth Circus. Because of his hard work, James became one of the youngest men ever to be promoted to the position of general agent. He was just 21.

While staying at a hotel in Bill Lake's hometown of Zanesville, Ohio, James met the hotel owner's daughter, Ruth Louisa McCaddon. They became friends, then fell in love. They were married in December of 1868.

Ruth's nine-year-old brother, Joe, begged James to take him along with the circus. James promised that when Joe was old enough to leave home, James would take Joe with him. Mr. Bailey was true to his word. After Joe grew up, he worked for James for many years.

In the meantime, Bill and Agnes' circus was heading for tragedy.

CIRCUS TERMS

HOUSE: Where the audience sits

JOEY: A clown

JUMP: The distance between towns

KIP: A name for a bed

In those days, many outlaws, conmen, and thieves followed the circuses, stealing and cheating people out of their money. On the night of August 21, 1869, in Granby, Missouri, one of those outlaws shot and killed Bill Lake.

James stayed with Agnes Lake's circus until the end of the season, then looked for work with another show. He found it with the company of Hemmings, Cooper, & Whitby. In just a few years, he became a full partner with James E. Cooper.

Under Bailey's management, the circus of Cooper, Bailey & Company quickly became a highly successful show. Then, in 1876, James got an idea for a bold plan. He wanted to take the entire circus on a tour of Australia, New Zealand, and South America. The circus had never been there before. But...would Mr. Cooper go along with his idea?

DID YOU KNOW?

After Bill Lake's death, Agnes Lake became the first woman in America to own a circus.

In 1876, she married famous gunfighter Wild Bill Hickok, who at one time worked with Buffalo Bill Cody. Years later, James Bailey helped manage Buffalo Bill's Wild West Show.

Wild Bill Hickok
1837-1876

5
AUSTRALIA!

Yes! Mr. Cooper thought it was risky, but he finally agreed. He didn't go along on the trip, but James brought his wife, Ruth, and her brother, Joe, with him on his new adventure.

What a sight it must have been that day on the docks of San Francisco! Cooper & Bailey's troupe of performers paraded down the walkway to board the steamship, *The City of Sydney*. Along with them came a menagerie of animals: lions, tigers, panthers, and leopards. Horses, monkeys, bears, jaguars, and snakes. Six elephants, five camels, one hippopotamus, one zebra, and one very tall giraffe.

The boat steamed out of the harbor on November 8, 1876, headed to the Hawaiian Islands, 2,393 miles away. People cheered as the boat entered the harbor at Honolulu. Even the king of Hawaii, King Kalakaua, came aboard the steamer for a visit. The company left the next day for the second part of their journey.

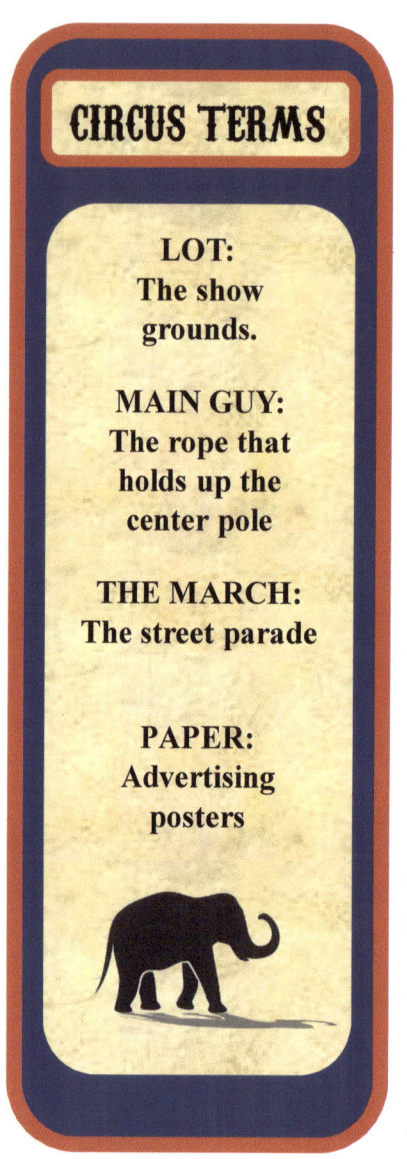

CIRCUS TERMS

LOT:
The show grounds.

MAIN GUY:
The rope that holds up the center pole

THE MARCH:
The street parade

PAPER:
Advertising posters

The show toured for two years in Australia. Joe McCaddon wrote in his diary that, "Mr. Bailey was everywhere acclaimed as an astute and highly successful showman...by the...officials, press and public..."

Cooper & Bailey's circus then headed for South America. On the way, they ran into a violent storm. The waves tossed the ship around so much that Joe was afraid it was going to capsize. He searched for James, only to find him lying in bed, calmly reading a book. He was completely confident that the ship's captain would take care of it, which he did!

When they returned to America, Cooper & Bailey bought another circus, Howe's Great London. In 1880, one of their newly acquired elephants gave birth. The baby elephant soon drew the attention of James' greatest competitor, the famous Phineas Taylor "P. T." Barnum.

DID YOU KNOW?

P. T. Barnum only spent a short period of his life as a circus owner. He was also a salesman, a politician, a museum owner, and a promoter. Barnum was 70 years old when he partnered with James Bailey, who was then just 34.

P. T. Barnum
1810-1891

6
ELEPHANTS!

The baby elephant's name was Columbia. Standing just three feet tall and weighing 213½ pounds, she was thought to be the first baby elephant born in captivity.

Bailey owned her. Barnum wanted her.

He offered Mr. Bailey a large sum of money for Columbia. But James refused the offer. Instead, he used it to advertise how much Barnum was willing to pay for her. More people flocked to Cooper & Bailey's show than to Barnum's, just to see the new little pachyderm.

Whether because of Columbia or because it made financial sense, Barnum and Bailey agreed to combine their two circuses. Between them, they owned twenty elephants!

In 1882, they added one more. They named him "Jumbo." He was destined to become one of the most famous elephants in the history of the circus.

Though Barnum usually gets credited with this purchase, it was actually James Bailey who arranged to buy Jumbo from the London Zoo.

In 1884, Barnum and Bailey put on a spectacular publicity event with Jumbo in New York. The Brooklyn Bridge was barely a year old, and people were still worried about how much weight it could hold. With Jumbo in the lead, 21 elephants and 17 camels paraded all the way across the bridge. It proved beyond a doubt how strong it was!

By 1886, James had spent most of his life in the circus world. He retired and built Ruth a mansion they named "The Knolls." Joe visited often and even lived with them for a while. But two years later, James returned, once again partnering with Barnum. Together, they would build one of the most famous and spectacular shows of its time.

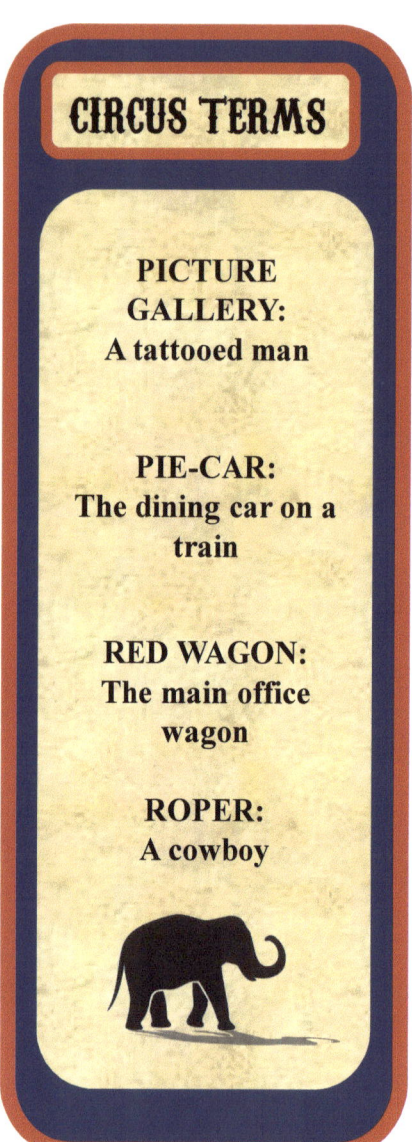

CIRCUS TERMS

PICTURE GALLERY:
A tattooed man

PIE-CAR:
The dining car on a train

RED WAGON:
The main office wagon

ROPER:
A cowboy

DID YOU KNOW?

Jumbo stood almost 12 feet tall and weighed 13,000 pounds. Every day, he ate 200 pounds of hay, a barrel of potatoes, two bushels of oats, and 15 loaves of bread.

WILD WEST

If P. T. Barnum was the famous face of the circus, James Anthony Bailey was the heart. He was at the circus from sunup to sundown, until every detail was handled, and everyone was settled in for the night.

Equestrienne Josie Demott Robinson, who performed on horseback for the circus, wrote that, "Mr. Barnum was the advertiser, who loved the limelight, who rode around in the ring, and announced who he was. But Mr. Bailey was the businessman, content to be invisible…and interested only in the success of the show."

He was such a hard worker that Barnum once wrote to him that James managed the show "ten times better than I could."

Bailey's outstanding management skills came in handy when the two bought the circus of a major competitor, Adam Forepaugh. Sadly, P. T. Barnum died not long afterward, on April 7, 1891, leaving Mr. Bailey to manage both of the circuses.

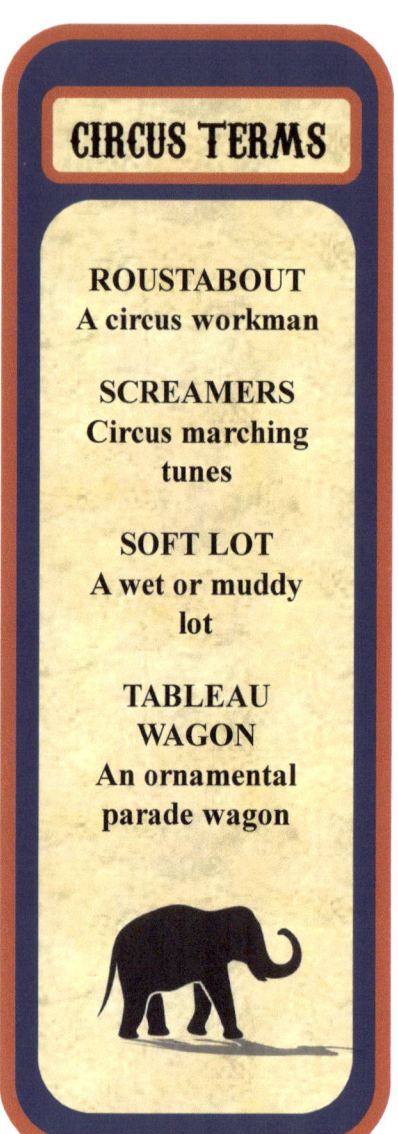

CIRCUS TERMS

ROUSTABOUT
A circus workman

SCREAMERS
Circus marching tunes

SOFT LOT
A wet or muddy lot

TABLEAU WAGON
An ornamental parade wagon

James was more than up to the task. He loved solving problems. The bigger the problem, the happier he was. "Can't do it" was not part of his vocabulary.

In 1894, he took on yet another major enterprise, Buffalo Bill Cody's Wild West Show.

Like P. T. Barnum, Buffalo Bill was a legend in his own time and a masterful showman. Also, like Barnum, he depended on others to run the day-to-day workings of his show.

And like the circus, the show featured performers, animals, and equipment. Transporting people, equipment, and animals efficiently was what James did best! He helped manage the Wild West Show for almost twelve years.

But then, one spring day, he got sick from an infection. About a week later, on April 11, 1906, James Anthony Bailey passed away.

DID YOU KNOW?

Buffalo Bill's Wild West Show was a spectacular depiction of life in the old West, complete with cowboys and cowgirls, Native Americans, horseback riding, sharpshooting, and buffalo hunting.

The show toured the United States and Europe for 30 years.

JAMES A. BAILEY AND COLONEL WM. F. CODY

Buffalo Bill Center of the West, Cody, Wyoming; McCracken Research Library; MS 288- General Photograph Collection; P.288.0116.

8 LEGACY

The death of James Anthony Bailey rocked the circus world. "James A. Bailey, King of Circus Men, is Dead," proclaimed the New York *Times* headline.

In his book about the circus, Earl Chapin May wrote, "Probably...no circus owner and manager left more sincere mourners than the thin little magnate known to millions as James A. Bailey."

Most of the people who knew James Bailey or worked with him liked and respected him. He was a quiet, private man who hardly ever raised his voice. If he did get upset, he would chew on rubber bands. Everyone knew not to bother him until he spit them out!

He was known to everyone, even P. T. Barnum, as "Mr. Bailey." Only Ruth and Joe called him "Jimmy," and then only in private.

He was not a big man, but he had a big impact on the circus world.

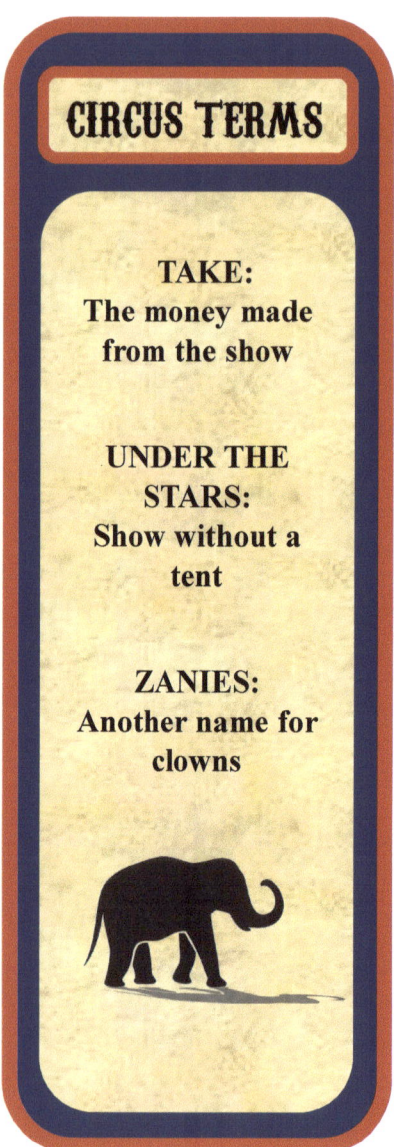

CIRCUS TERMS

TAKE:
The money made from the show

UNDER THE STARS:
Show without a tent

ZANIES:
Another name for clowns

James had protected his circusgoers for years by hiring Pinkerton detectives to keep the grifters and thieves away.

His genius with organizing and moving animals, people and equipment was copied by the military of more than one country.

He often gave people money when they were in need, and he always treated his animals as well as his people.

Taped below a photo of James in the scrapbook of Harrison Gunning, an employee, is a small piece of paper that reads, "P. T. Barnum was the great showman, but Mr. Bailey was the supreme of all circus managers, past and present."

It is a fitting tribute to the boy who started down that road so many years before, barefoot and alone, and grew up to become the owner of The Greatest Show on Earth.

DID YOU KNOW?

The Pinkerton National Detective Agency was established in 1850 by detective Allan Pinkerton.

In 1856, he made history by hiring the first female detective in the United States, Kate Warne.

Allan Pinkerton (seated on right) during the Civil War.

AUTHOR NOTE

The arrival of the circus in towns across America in the 19th century was a major event. There were no televisions, radios, computers, social media, or movie theaters. It was not unexpected that James Bailey, given his strong work ethic, determination, and integrity, would rise to fame in one of the country's biggest businesses.

Journalist and co-worker, George O. Starr, wrote, "Mr. Bailey is a good man and a great man…Chance made him a showman, but he would have been equally great in whatever place his lines might have fallen."

James was highly intelligent and always looking for opportunities and new innovations. When the electric lightbulb was a fairly new invention, James was the first to use electric lights inside the circus tent.

His friend Peter McNally said about James that, "His watchword was work; and that, with his great brain and his energy and attention to detail, were the secrets of his success."

Although P. T. Barnum gets most of the credit for the success of their circus, it's a testament to James Bailey's abilities that he continued to run the Greatest Show on Earth successfully for fifteen years following Barnum's death.

Joe McCaddon, his brother-in-law and probably James Bailey's biggest fan, knew him better than almost anyone. So, it was not surprising to find a note scribbled on the margin of Joe's diary that reads,

"Bailey, not Barnum, Master Showman of the World."

ACKNOWLEDGEMENTS

With special thanks to...

My stellar, talented, and long-suffering critique partners and friends who kept me going to finish this book: Jean, Joan, Charlie, Lisa, Laurie, Gloria, Kate, Lana, Vera and Margaret; my husband and captive audience, Jim; Paul Adams for tech support, and especially, to one other critique partner and friend, author LeeAnn Blankenship, who first sparked my interest in the history of the circus, which led to my interest in telling the story of James Anthony Bailey.

Also, to...

Elizabeth Van Tuyl of Bridgeport Public Library, and Thomas Warren of Kent State University Library, two librarians without whose research this book would not have been possible; to Nic Ellis for his support and information about sutlers; to Mary Robinson and Mack Frost of McCracken Research Library; to Mark Schmitt of Milner Library; and to Ray Lucas of the Oakland County Pioneer Historical Society.

James A. Bailey Timeline

1847-James Anthony McGinnis born, July 4, Detroit, Michigan

1849-Father, Edward McGinnis, dies, October, of cholera

1855-Mother, Hannora McGinnis, dies, August 1. James goes to live with his sister, Catherine Gordon

1859 or 1860-Runs away from home

*1861-Joins the Robinson & Lake Circus/changes last name to Bailey

1863-Becomes a sutler's clerk during the Civil War

1866-After the Civil War ends, returns to circus life as agent for William Lake's circus

1868-Marries Ruth Louisa McCaddon

1869-William Lake shot and killed

1870-Becomes part of the Hemmings & Cooper circus

1873-Buys out Hemmings

1875-Goes into partnership with Cooper

1876-1878-Takes Cooper and Bailey show to Australia, New Zealand, South America

1878-Buys Great London Circus and Sanger's Royal British Menagerie

*Though many sources cite 1860 as the year Bailey left Pontiac, Michigan, with the circus, the Robinson & Lake Route Sheets record that the circus didn't play in Pontiac until 1861.

1880-Baby elephant "Columbia" born in captivity with Cooper & Bailey Circus

1881-Forms partnership with P.T. Barnum and James L. Hutchinson

1882-Buys Jumbo from England

1886-1888-Retires and builds his mansion, The Knolls

1888-Returns to work as an equal partner with Barnum

1890-Buys Adam Forepaugh Circus

1891-Barnum dies, April 7

1894-Bailey becomes sole owner of Barnum & Bailey Circus and forms management agreement with Buffalo Bill Cody's Wild West Show

1896-Buys one-third of the Sells Brothers Circus and takes B & B show to London

1898-1902-Takes show on European Tour

1904-Signs agreement with Ringling Brothers Circus to divide sections of America for touring

1905-Sells one-half ownership in Forepaugh Circus to the Ringling Brothers

1906-Bailey dies at The Knolls, April 11

1907-Ruth Bailey sells the Barnum and Bailey circus to the Ringling Brothers

1960-James A. Bailey inducted into the International Circus Hall of Fame

1991- James A. Bailey Inducted into the Circus Ring of Fame, Sarasota, FL

SOURCE NOTES

Page 2: McCaddon, James M. *Memoir*. Papers of James McCaddon (BHC-MSS 0008). Bridgeport History Center, Bridgeport CT., p.4

Pages 3 and 6: Ibid. pgs.9-10

Page 7: Ibid. p.10

Page 19: Ibid. p. 62

Page 26: Robinson, Josephine Demott. *The Circus Lady*. Thomas Y. Crowell, New York, NY,1926, p.153.

Page 26: Fleming, Candace. *The Great and Only Barnum The Tremendous, Stupendous Life of Showman P.T. Barnum*. Schwartz & Wade, 2009. p.113

Page 30: *James A. Bailey, King of Circus Men, Is Dead*. New York Times, 12 Apr. 1906, headline.

Page 30: May, Earl Chapin. *The Circus from Rome to Ringling*. Duffield and Green, 1932, p. 171.

Page 31: Scrapbook of Harrison Gunning, William F. Cody Scrapbooks, McCracken Research Library, Buffalo Bill Center of the West, Cody, Wyoming. MS6.3678.023.00.

Page 33: Allen, Whiting. *Captains of Industry: James Anthony Bailey*. The Cosmopolitan (1886-1907). December, 1902.

Page 33: Slout, William L. *A Royal Coupling: The Historic Marriage of Barnum and Bailey*. Borgo Press, 2000.

Page 34: McCaddon, James M. *Memoir*. Papers of James McCaddon (BHC-MSS 0008). Bridgeport History Center, Bridgeport CT., p.68.

Page 34 : Ibid. p.211.

Circus Terms:
International Circus Hall of Fame, Glossary of Circus Terminology. Visit.circushalloffame.com/glossary-of-circus-terminology/

American Circus Lingo, goodmagic.com/carny/c_a.htm

PHOTO CREDITS

Posters
Cover and Title page: Library of Congress, Public Domain. Courtesy of Wikimedia Commons.

Intro photo J. A. Bailey, black & white: By Strobridge Lith. Co. - https://www.flickr.com/photos/boston_public_library/6554391035, Public Domain. Courtesy of Wikimedia Commons

Pages 1, 5, 13, 21, 24, 29: Public Domain. Courtesy of Wikimedia Commons.

Page 9: By Strobridge & Co. Lith. - Library of Congress, Public Domain, Courtesy of Wikimedia Commons.

Page 17: Library of Congress, Public Domain. Courtesy of Wikimedia Commons.

Page 25: By The Strobridge Litho. Co., Cincinnati & New York. - Library of Congress[1], Public Domain,

Photos:
Page 12, **Sutler's Tent:** By Civil War Glass Negatives - Library of Congress, Public Domain. Courtesy of Wikimedia Commons.

Page 20, **P.T. Barnum:** By unattributed - Harvard Library, Public Domain.
Courtesy of Wikimedia Commons.

Page 16, **Wild Bill Hickok:** Public Domain, Courtesy of Wikimedia Commons.

Page 32, **Pinkerton Detectives:** By Spalm jhu at English Wikipedia - https://www.cia.gov/library/publications/additional-publications/civil-war/SML.htm, Public Domain. Courtesy of Wikimedia Commons.

BIBLIOGRAPHY

Books

Bradna, Fred, and Hartzell Spence. *The Big Top: My Forty Years with the Greatest Show on Earth*. Hamish Hamilton, 1953.

Bryan III, J. *The World's Greatest Showman.* Random House, 1956.

Conklin, George, and Harvey W. Root. *The Ways of the Circus: Being the Memories and Adventures of George Conklin, Tamer of Lions.* Harper, 1921.

Fisher, Linda A., and Carrie Bowers. *Agnes Lake Hickok: Queen of the Circus, Wife of a Legend.* University of Oklahoma Press: Norman, 2009.

Fleming, Candace. *The Great and Only Barnum The Tremendous, Stupendous Life of Showman P.T. Barnum*. Schwartz & Wade, 2009.

Kotar, S. L., and J. E. Gessler. *The Rise of the American Circus, 1716-1899.* McFarland & Co., 2011.

Kunhardt, Philip B., *P.T. Barnum: America's Greatest Showman.* Alfred A. Knopf, Inc., 1995.

May, Earl Chapin. *The Circus from Rome to Ringling*. Duffield and Green, 1932. pages 119-127, 170-172

Robinson, Josephine Demott. *The Circus Lady*. Thomas Y. Crowell, New York, NY, 1926.

Saxon, A. H. *P.T. Barnum: The Legend and the Man*. Columbia University Press, 1989.

Slout, William L. *A Royal Coupling: The Historic Marriage of Barnum and Bailey*. Borgo Press, 2000.

Springhall, J. *Genesis of Mass Culture: Show Business Live in America 1840 to 1940*. Palgrave Macmillan, 2016.

Tobey, John E. & Nicolas H. Ellis. *U.S. Army Sutler, 1861-1865*. Milatus Publications, 2012.

Pamphlets, Websites, and Newspaper Articles

A Caesar Among Showmen: James A. Bailey the Partner and Successor of Barnum. New York Times, April 19, 1891.

Albrecht, Ernest. *Bailey, James Anthony (1847-1906), Circus Owner.* American National Biography. Philosophical Transactions of the Royal Society B: Biological Sciences, The Royal Society, 16 June 2017.

Allen, Whiting. *Captains of Industry: James Anthony Bailey.* The Cosmopolitan (1886-1907). December, 1902.

America's Big Circus Spectacular Has a Long and Cherished History. Smithsonian.com, Smithsonian Institution, 22 Mar. 2017.

Bowers, Liz. *This is Not a Circus!: James A. Bailey Redefines Buffalo Bill's Wild West Show.* 27 March, 2019.

Conover, Richard E., *The Affairs of James A. Bailey: New Revelations on the Career of the World's Most Successful Showman,* 1957.

DeLong, William. *How Jumbo the Elephant Went from "The Greatest Show on Earth" to a University Mascot,* December, 2017. https://allthatsinteresting.com/jumbo-the-elephant

History of Circus Co-Founder James A. Bailey. Detroit Free Press, April 12, 1906.

James A. Bailey, King of Circus Men, Is Dead. New York Times, 12 Apr. 1906.

James Anthony Bailey. P.T. Barnum, History and Information, Circuses and Sideshows.

Kelly, Kate. *James A. Bailey.* Westchester County Historical Society.

McCaddon, James M. *Memoir.* Papers of James McCaddon (BHC-MSS 0008). Bridgeport History Center, Bridgeport CT.

Middleton, George. *Circus Memoirs.* Sideshow World.

The Elelphants Cross the Bridge. New York Times, May 18, 1884.

The Show World Emperor. James A. Bailey, the Partner and Successor of P.T. Barnum. Philadelphia Inquirer, Oct 13, 1891.

INDEX

Australia, 15, 19

Bailey, Colonel, 6, 7

Barnum, P. T., 19, 20, 22, 23, 26, 27

Cody, Buffalo Bill, 16, 27, 28

Columbia, 22

Cooper, James E., 15, 18, 19

Detroit, MI, 2

Forepaugh, Adam, 26

Green, A. H., 10, 11

Jumbo, 22, 23

Lake, Agnes, 14, 15, 16

Lake, Bill, 7, 11, 14, 15

McCaddon, Joe, 14, 18, 19, 23, 30

McCaddon, Ruth, 14, 18, 23, 30

Nashville, TN, 10

Orphan Day, 4, 27

Pinkerton, Allan, 31, 32

Pontiac, MI, 6, 7

Sutlers, 10, 11

ABOUT THE AUTHOR

Gloria G. Adams spent most of her career as a children's librarian and storyteller.

She has been published in books and magazines and has two picture books published: ***Ah-Choo!*** with co-author Lana Wayne Koehler, Sterling Children's Books, 2016, and ***My Underpants are Made from Plants***, with co-author Vera J. Hurst, originally published through Schoolwide, Inc., 2015.

She has written books for Rosen, Enslow, and Greenhaven Press, and has published through her independent publishing company, Slanted Ink. She also is partner in a manuscript editing company with author, Jean Daigneau, Two-4-One Kid Critiques, LLC.

Learn more about Gloria on her website:
www.gloriagadams.com

While discrepancies are frequently found when doing historical research, I have verified the information presented in this book to the best of my ability. Accuracy is dependent on the sources who originally penned the information.

~Gloria G. Adams

www.ingramcontent.com/pod-product-compliance
Lightning Source LLC
Chambersburg PA
CBHW042255100526
44589CB00002B/21